Smythe Gambrell Library

Dedicated to the Glory of God
and
Presented in Loving Memory
of
Mr. and Mrs. Carlyle Fraser
Beloved Benefactors and Friends

ABINGDON'S
Bible Handbook
for
Young Readers

A guide to help you read it for yourself

Published in the United States of America by Abingdon Press, 201 Eighth Avenue, South, P.O. Box 801, Nashville, Tennessee 37202-0801.

ISBN 0-687-00809-3

Manufactured in Singapore

ABINGDON'S
Bible Handbook for Young Readers

HOLY
BIBLE

Written and illustrated by
Richard and Christine Deverell

CONT

ENTS

What is the Bible?

On the cover of every Bible it says, 'Holy Bible'. This is because the Bible is a very special book. It tells a long story, made up of many shorter stories, of how God, the Creator of the universe, made people, and how God wanted these people to be like him.

It is through the Bible that God speaks to us today. When we read it, we are 'tapping in' to God's thoughts. In the last two thousand years, the Bible has changed many people's thinking, and in turn, changed their lives.

"Just as the heavens are higher than the earth,
So are my ways higher than your ways.
And my thoughts are higher than your thoughts."
Isaiah 55:9

The Bible is not one book, but a collection of 66 books. These are the books in the order they appear in the Bible. The 39 books of the Old Testament are in four groups.

The 27 books of the New Testament include The Gospels with Acts [history letters from the Apostles to the churches, and Revelation which is a prophecy.

The Bible had many different writers, and we know who some of them were.

Who? When? Where?

The Old Testament tells the story of Israel, a Semitic nation in the Middle East. This story begins with Abraham about 2000 years BC [Before Christ],

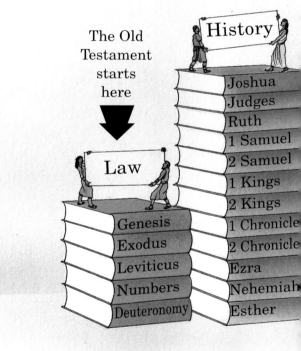

The Old Testament starts here

History

Joshua
Judges
Ruth
1 Samuel
2 Samuel
1 Kings
2 Kings
1 Chronicle
2 Chronicle
Ezra
Nehemiah
Esther

Law

Genesis
Exodus
Leviticus
Numbers
Deuteronomy

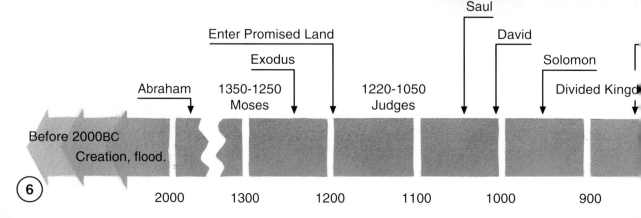

Enter Promised Land

Exodus

Saul

David

Solomon

Abraham · 1350-1250 Moses · 1220-1050 Judges · Divided Kingd

Before 2000BC
Creation, flood.

2000   1300   1200   1100   1000   900

when civilisations like Egypt were very strong, but nomadic tribes were moving from place to place in the deserts. The Israelites settled in a land of their own and became an important nation.

The New Testament covers a period of about 100 years from the birth of Jesus and throughout the lives of the Apostles. These events took place in Palestine and the Roman Empire.

The Bible is a lot more than a history book. It tells the story of God's relationship with the human beings he created. God chose Abraham to be the father of the nation, Israel. The Bible shows us what God is like, and how we can know him.

Letters

Romans
1 Corinthians
2 Corinthians
Galatians
Ephesians
Philippians
Colossians
1 Thessalonians
2 Thessalonians
1 Timothy
2 Timothy
Titus
Philemon
Hebrews
James
1 Peter
2 Peter
1 John
2 John
3 John
Jude

Prophecy

Isaiah
Jeremiah
Lamentations
Ezekiel
Daniel
Hosea
Joel
Amos
Obadiah
Jonah
Micah
Nahum
Habakkuk
Zephaniah
Haggai
Zechariah
Malachi

The New Testament starts here

↓

History

Matthew
Mark
Luke
John
Acts

Wisdom

Job
Psalms
Proverbs
Ecclesiastes
Song of Songs

Prophecy

Revelation

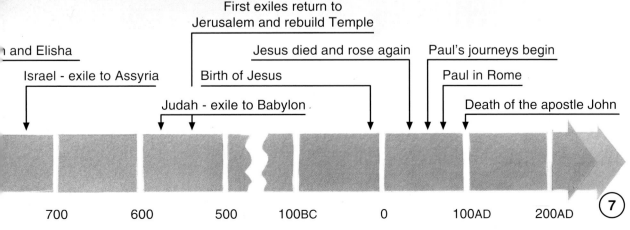

First exiles return to Jerusalem and rebuild Temple

and Elisha

Israel - exile to Assyria

Jesus died and rose again

Paul's journeys begin

Birth of Jesus

Paul in Rome

Judah - exile to Babylon

Death of the apostle John

700   600   500   100BC   0   100AD   200AD

How to use this book

At the beginning of each chapter of this book you will see pictures of one or more books. These are the books in the Bible where you will find the stories, prophecies or letters that you'll read about in the chapter. In this book you will find the Bible books in the place where they fit in history - not necessarily in the order that they appear in the Bible.

Your Bible

You will find it useful to have a Bible to look at while you are reading this book. There are many different translations of the Bible. Some are easier to understand than others. Most have VERY small type - smaller than the other books you read. Some Bibles have pictures, but there's not room for many.

So reading the Bible can be hard work. We hope this book makes it easier for you. The Bible translation that we have used in this book is the International Children's Bible, New Century Version [Nelson Word]. The paragraphs that you read in bold type are the words taken from the Bible. These will be followed by a **reference** in italics. This tells you where in the Bible you will find the words.

God promised this Good News long ago through his prophets. That promise is written in the Holy Scriptures.

Romans 1:2

Read it yourself

Throughout this book you will see the word **Read**, followed by a **Bible reference.** We might be telling you to read a whole story; or a short passage that will help you to understand something better.

You will get to know your Bible if you stop and **READ**.

You might have a book of **Bible stories**. There are many that you can buy or borrow from the library. These books will introduce you to the people of the Bible and the stories about them.

Finding your place

Somewhere at the beginning of your Bible you will find a page of **Contents**. This lists all the books in order and tells you the page where each book begins.

Each book in the Bible is divided into **chapters.** Open your Bible anywhere. At the top of each page you will find the name of the book and the chapter number.

Each chapter is divided into **verses.** To point the way to **one verse** we need directions to find the **book,** the **chapter,** and the **verse:**

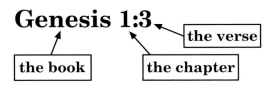

If we want you to read a whole chapter, then the reference looks like this:
Genesis 2 OR **Genesis chapter 2**

The book of Psalms is not divided into chapters. Each Psalm has a number. You say "Psalm four".

Find **Psalm 119:2**

Some of the New Testament letters only have one chapter. Find **Jude verse 24.**

When you need to find more than one verse, you will see a reference like this:

Genesis 2:1-3

Here you need to find the book of **Genesis**, chapter **2**, and read from the beginning of verse **1** to the end of verse **3**.

A reference with a comma.
Genesis 2:18,21-22
Find **Genesis chapter 2**. Read verse **18**. [Skip 19 and 20]. Then read verses **21** and **22**.

Beginnings

**GENESIS
EXODUS
LEVITICUS
NUMBERS
DEUTERONOMY**

The word 'Genesis' means 'beginning', and the book of Genesis tells us about many beginnings:

the beginning of the world
the beginning of life
a new beginning after
the great flood and
the small beginning
of a great nation -

ISRAEL!

Genesis is the first of five books in the Old Testament which tell the story of the early part of Israel's history. They were written to remind the people of Israel how they began, and how God wanted them to live by obeying his laws. As we shall see, sometimes they remembered, and sometimes they forgot!

The beginning of the universe

The first thing that we learn about God from the Bible is this: God is the creator - the one who made it all.

In the beginning God created the sky and the earth. The earth was empty and had no form. Darkness covered the ocean, and God's Spirit was moving over the water.

Genesis 1:1-2

We see from the first chapter of Genesis how God **spoke**, and the world as we know it came to be. God said,

'Let there be light!' And there was light. God saw that the light was good.

Genesis 1:3,4

In the same way the sun, moon and stars, and the land and seas were put in their places.

Plant life appeared on the earth, and God gave orders that the plants should make seeds, to make more plants grow!

Next, God created the animal kingdom . . . and all of them were to produce more of their own kind.

What a mess!

The first man was called Adam, and the first woman was called Eve. God gave them a garden to live in - the Garden of Eden.

God told Adam that he could eat any fruit from any tree in the garden, except one.

A snake came and tempted Eve.

She ate the fruit . . .

. . . and gave the fruit to Adam to eat.

Adam and Eve had disobeyed God. So God sent them away from the garden.

But the best was to come!

Then God said, "Let us make human beings in our image and likeness. . . Let them rule over the tame animals, over all the earth and over all the small crawling animals on the earth."

So God created human beings in his image. In the image of God he created them. He created them male and female.

Genesis 1:26,27

You will find this story in Genesis chapter 3. Everything changed when Adam and Eve did the very thing God told them not to do. Before, they were God's friends. Now they were separated from God. From now on this is the BIG problem! This is what the Bible calls SIN, and sin is what stops us from being God's friends.

The Bible tells us how we can become God's friends again. Because God has always loved us, he made it possible. God sent Jesus to die for our sins, so that we can be really alive in the way God meant us to be from the beginning. You can read about this in the New Testament - in the letter of Paul to the Romans, chapter 5.

So one sin of Adam brought the punishment of death to all people. But in the same way, one good act that Christ did makes all people right with God. And that brings true life for all.

Romans 5:18

Noah
and the
great flood

People became very bad, and this made God very unhappy. God began to wish that he had never made them. When he looked around the earth, God could only find one good man - Noah.

God told Noah to build a very large boat. It had to be big enough to carry all of Noah's family, as well as two of every land animal and bird - one male and one female. For God was going to send a flood, and he wanted Noah's family and all the animals to be safe.

For 40 days it rained, and the earth was flooded. Noah's family lived in the boat with all the animals for more than a year!

When the flood water dried up, they all left the boat, and God made a promise.

"I am putting my rainbow in the clouds. It is the sign of the agreement between me and the earth. . . . Flood waters will never again destroy all life on the earth."

Genesis 9:13,15

Read

Why did God send the flood
Genesis 6:1-8

Noah built the boat
Genesis 6:9-22

Down came the ra
Genesis chapter

The flood waters dried up
Genesis chapter 8

Rescue!

Noah and his family were saved from the flood and had a new start in life. In the New Testament we are told how Jesus died to rescue us. We can also have a new life, because Jesus was raised from death. The Apostle Peter wrote:

Christ himself died for you. And that one death paid for your sins. He was not guilty, but he died for those who are guilty. He did this to bring you all to God. His body was killed, but he was made alive in the spirit.

1 Peter 3:1

Abraham

a man who trusted God . . .

The nation of Israel began with one man - Abraham. He lived with his father in the city of Ur, in Sumer. The whole family later moved to Haran. When Abraham's father died, God said to him,

"Leave your country, your relatives and your father's family. Go to the land that I will show you."

Genesis 12:1

Abraham was 75 years old when he left his home. He had no idea where God would lead him.

God's promise to Abraham

"I will make you a great nation, and I will bless you. I will make you famous and you will be a blessing to others."

Genesis 12:2

What's in a name?

Abraham's old name was Abram. God gave him the new name, **Abraham** which means **'father of many nations'**.

Sarah means **'princess'**.

Isaac means **'laughter'**. This is because Sarah laughed and said, 'Everyone will laugh with me.'

God promised that a great nation would come from Abraham.

Problem! Abraham and his wife Sarah were old. They did not have any children!

The promised son . . .

Abraham, You will have a son of your own. Your descendants will be too many to count, like the stars in the sky.

Don't be silly. I'm much too old to have a baby.

It was the custom in those days, if a woman was not able to have a baby, then a slave could have a baby for her.

My slave girl, Hagar, can have a baby. Then you will have the son that God promised you.

A year later . . .

Ishmael is born.

13 years later . . .

Abraham, I promised you a son. From him will come a great nation.

Sarah is much too old. Please let Ishmael be the child of your promise.

No, Abraham. A great nation **will** come from Ishmael. But Sarah's son, Isaac, will be the son of my promise.

Ha, ha, ha, ha, ha . .

No one thought I would have a baby, but I have given Abraham a son in his old age.

Abraham was 100 years old when Isaac was born. Sarah was 99!

Abraham left Haran with his family to make the journey south. They were not poor people. They took many servants with them, and Abraham owned large numbers of sheep, cattle, camels and donkeys.

In the towns, they had houses to live in. But now they were moving from place to place across the desert, and lived in tents. Some people still live like this today in the Middle East.

A wife for Isaac

When Isaac grew up, Abraha[m] sent a servant to find a wife [for] him. He did not want his son [to] marry a stranger from Cana[an.]

The Promised Land

Abraham became rich in Egypt. Back in Canaan God said,

"Look all around you. Look north and south and east and west. All this land that you see I will give you and your descendants for ever."

Genesis 13:14-15

There's food in Egypt!

Abraham arrived in the land of Canaan. Usually much food grew there, but when Abraham got to Canaan, there was a famine in the land. So Abraham continued on to Egypt.

It was about 1900BC and many refugees from Canaan found their way to Egypt, where there was a good supply of food.

An important man in Egypt had a picture painted on his tomb, showing a group of travellers from Canaan.

e told the servant to go to Haran, here he found a wife for Isaac om Abraham's family. Her name as Rebekah.

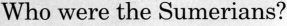

Sumerians were farmers and grew of food. They took and vegetables to old in the city kets.

Who were the Sumerians?

The Sumerians and the Semites [Abraham's race] came to live in Mesopotamia - 'the land between two rivers' in about 3000BC. It is part of the modern country of Iraq.

The Sumerians were very clever. They built cities like Ur and Haran, and dams and canals to control the rivers. Children went to school, where they learned to write using a kind of picture writing. They also learned mathematics, which helped them learn about the stars.

Sumerians counted in tens and sixties. They invented the time system that we use today - 60 seconds in a minute, and 60 minutes in an hour. They divided a circle into 360 degrees.

Find Genesis 22:1-18

Read this story about Abraham and Isaac. It tells how God tested Abraham's faith. Abraham knew that God would not let Isaac die.

Read Genesis 17:19 and see why Abraham was so sure.

A baby for Sarah
Genesis 21:1-5

Three visitors
Genesis 18:1-16

Abraham's journey
Genesis 12:4-9

Adventures in Egypt
Genesis 12:10-20

What happened to Ishmael?
Genesis 21:8-20

Is this the promised son?
Genesis 16:1-16

Fathers and Sons

A family tree

Abraham's family grew like this

Abraham
married
Sarah

Isaac
married
Rebekah

Esau and **Jacob**

The life of Joseph is one of the most exciting stories in the Bible.

There is a lot to read here! Don't try to read it all at once . . . just a chunk a day.

Read

That's cheating!

Esau and Jacob were twins, and Esau was born first. The firstborn son usually got most of the father's riches, and became the leader of the family when the father died. But Jacob tricke his brother. One day when Esau was very hungry he asked Jacob for some soup. Jacob said, "You must sell me your rights as the firstborn son."

Genesis 37:5-17

Joseph was a dreamer. He dreamed that his brothers would one day bow down to him.

Genesis 37:18-36

They decided to kill him . . . but see how he came to be in Egypt.

Genesis 39

I'm putting you in charge of everything I own

What happened to Joseph in Egypt ?

Read **Genesis chapter 27** to see how Jacob tricked his father, Isaac, who was old and nearly blind. Jacob dressed up to look like Esau. Rebekah helped him. She put goat's hair on Jacob's hands so that he would feel hairy like his brother. Isaac was fooled! He gave Jacob the blessing that he really wanted Esau to have. The promise that God made to Abraham passed to Jacob and his children.

Esau was angry, and planned to kill his brother, so Jacob set off to Haran to find a wife.

14 years of hard work!

Back in Haran, Jacob found his mother's brother, Laban. Jacob loved his cousin Rachel, and promised to work for his uncle for seven years if Laban would let him marry her.

Read Genesis **29:21-30** and see how Jacob ended up with two wives! And worked for **14** years!

12 sons for Jacob!

Life was not easy for Jacob with two wives. He loved Rachel, but she did not have any children for a long time. When Jacob already had ten sons, Rachel gave birth to a son and named him Joseph.

Joseph was his father's favorite.

He made Joseph a special robe with long sleeves. Joseph's brothers saw that their father loved Joseph more than he loved them. So they hated their brother and could not speak to him politely.

Genesis 37:3,4

Genesis 40-41

...d how did he become a ...ler in that land?

Genesis 42-45

Joseph's dreams came true!

Genesis 46:1-7

And all Jacob's family came to live in Egypt.

Slaves in EGYPT

Jacob's family stayed in Egypt, in the land called Goshen. They were always strangers to the Egyptians, and were called 'Israelites'. 70 people left Canaan for Egypt. After about 400 years there were so many Israelites in Egypt that the king was afraid of them. He decided to make them his slaves, and used them to build new cities.

The baby in the basket

Moses was an Israelite baby. He was born at a time when the king ordered that all baby Israelite boys were to be killed. His mother put him in a basket, and hid him in the reeds on the edge of the River Nile.

Moses was found by the king's daughter, and taken to live in the palace.

You can read this story in **Exodus 2:1-10**.

Life was very hard for the Israelites.

They had to work long hours in the hot sun. Some of them made bricks from mud and straw.

Others had to build huge storehouses, and fine houses for the Egyptians.

Some of them were put to work in the fields.

Their Egyptian masters treated them badly, and forced them to work very hard.

But they all had good food to eat.

Remember!

The promises God made to Abraham:

A great nation.
And here they are - thousands of them.

A land of their own.
But they are slaves in Egypt.

Read Exodus 2:11-25
See what happened to Moses when he grew up. He had to leave Egypt. Why?

Moses the leader

He escaped to the land of Midian where he worked for a man called Jethro. Moses married Zipporah - Jethro's daughter.

One day, Moses was looking after his father-in-law's sheep. He saw a bush on fire, and went to have a closer look . . .

Moses, Moses!

Here I am.

Do not come any closer. . . I am the God of Abraham, the God of Isaac, and the God of Jacob.

I have seen the troubles my people have suffered in Egypt. I have come down to save them from the Egyptians. I am sending you to the king of Egypt. Go! Bring my people, the Israelites out of Egypt!

I will be with you. But I know that the king of Egypt will not let you go. Only a great power will force him to let you go. So I will use my power against Egypt. After I do this, He will let you go.

Who made man's mouth? It is I, the Lord. Now go! I will tell you what to say.

Please, send someone else.

I am not a great man! Why should I be the one to go to the king and lead the Israelites out of Egypt?

But Lord, I am not a skilled speaker. I speak slowly, and can't find the best words.

Your brother Aaron is a skilled speaker. I will help both of you know what to say and do.

Escape from

Exodus

Moses and his brother, Aaron, went to the king of Egypt. They asked him to let the Israelites leave Egypt. The king said, "No!" So God sent disasters to Egypt. He wanted to show the king that he was a powerful God. The Israelites were God's own people and he would save them.

1
All the water turned to blood

2
The land was filled with frogs . . .

3
. . . then gnats .

10 These disasters happened all over Egypt but they did not happen in the place where the Israelites lived. When these disasters happened, the king sometimes called Moses and asked him to pray to God to make them stop. The king even promised to let the people go, but then he broke his promise.

The Passover

Pass over what?

So after the ninth disaster, Moses told the people to get ready to leave.

This is what they did. Each man got a lamb for his family to eat. They killed the lamb, and put some of its blood on the sides and tops of the door frames.

The whole lamb was roasted on the fire.

In the night, the eldest son in every Egyptian household died. But the Israelites were safe.

The king called for Moses and Aaron.

Get up and leave my people. You and your people may do as you have asked. . . Go.

The Egyptians gave the people rich gifts.

Please hurry! If you don't leave, we shall all die!

EGYPT

4
. . . and
hen flies.

5
Animals
became sick
and died

6
Animals and
people were
covered in
boils

7
A storm
destroyed the
crops

8
Locusts ate
all the plants

9
There was
darkness for
three days

God is sending another disaster. In one night all the firstborn sons, animals as well as people, will die. But when God sees the blood on your houses, he will pass over you. No one will be hurt.

The people sat down with their coats and sandals on, ready to leave. They ate the meat with herbs and bread made without yeast.

You are always to remember this day. Celebrate it with a feast to the Lord. Your descendants are to honor the Lord with this feast from now on.

Exodus 12:14

Crossing the sea

God led the Israelites through the desert towards the Red Sea. The king of Egypt sent his army to chase them and make them go back. But God took care of his people.

When they reached the sea, God told Moses,

Raise your staff and hold it over the sea. The sea will split. Then the people can cross the sea on dry land.

Exodus 14:16

When the people were safe on the other side, the water became deep again. The king's army were all drowned.

When the people of Israel saw the great power that the Lord had used against the Egyptians, they feared the Lord. And they trusted the Lord and his servant Moses.

Exodus 14:31

Laws and Promises

Leviticus Exodus Numbers Deuteronomy

Kadesh-barnea

Goshen

Ez
ge

Mount Sinai

Moses led the people of Israel safely through the desert to the Promised Land. They did not follow the quickest route. The whole journey took them 40 years!

Life in the desert

The Israelites lived in tents as they traveled, and God provided them with food and water.

Sometimes the camp was covered with **quails.**

Every morning God sent them **manna** to eat.

This is all they ate for 40 years!

Find the story in **Exodus 16:11-18**

Numbers is a book of numbers. It tells the story of the journey through the desert, but there was a lot of counting! Read Numbers chapter 1.

The Ten Commandments

When the Israelites reached Mount Sinai, God gave Moses the laws that he wanted them to obey. You can read the **Ten Commandments** in **Exodus 20:1-17**. There are more laws that you can read about in Exodus, and the book called **Leviticus** is full of laws.

Deuteronomy also has the laws, but in this book you can read more of the **promises** God gave his people. **Read Deuteronomy 5:33**

The Holy Tent
Exodus 36:8-38

The most important promise God made to his people was that he would always be with them.

The Israelites made a Holy Tent for the Lord. This is what it looked like.

Why 40 years?

Moses sent 12 men into the Promised Land to see what it was like there. You will know what they found if you read **Numbers 13:23-33.**

Numbers 14:1-4 will tell you what the Israelites said. They wished they had never left Egypt!

And **God** said,

"All these men saw my glory. They saw the miracles I did in Egypt and in the desert. But they disobeyed me and tested me ten times. So not one will see the land I promised to their ancestors. No one who angered me will see that land."

Numbers 14:22-23

Priests

Moses' brother Aaron, and Aaron's sons were made priests.

Priests were in charge of making the sacrifices.

Only Aaron, the high priest could go into the Most Holy Place in the Meeting Tent where he could meet God.

Levites - men from the tribe of Levi who helped the priests. They carried the Meeting Tent when the Israelites moved from place to place.

Today we do not need a special place to worship God. We do not need priests to speak to God for us. We can speak to him ourselves, wherever we are!

You can read about all these things in the New Testament, in Hebrews 9:1-22.

We can enter through a new way that Jesus opened for us. . . So let us come near to God with a sincere heart and a sure faith. . . We can trust God to do what he promised.

Hebrews 10:20,22,23

Sins and sacrifices

At the entrance to the Holy Tent, Moses put an altar for burning sacrifices. Animals had to be killed because of the sins of the people. The life of the animal was given to God in place of the life of the sinner who ought to have been punished. God forgave people for their sins in this way.

When Jesus died on the cross many hundreds of years later, he became the sacrifice for the sins of everyone. He was punished in our place, and no more sacrifices will ever be needed.

The Holy Ark

The stone tablets on which the Ten Commandments were written were kept in this special box.

The Promised

Moses died and Joshua became the leader. God promised Joshua:

Just as I was with Moses, so I will be with you. No one will be able to stop you all your life. I will not leave you. I will never leave you alone.

Joshua 1:5

Jericho

Jericho was an important city with strong walls. It was near the place where the Israelites crossed the River Jordan. Before they entered Canaan Joshua sent spies to Jericho to see how easy it would be to take the city.

READ the story of the spies in **Joshua chapter 2.**

God was with Joshua and the Israelites. They marched round the walls of Jericho once every day for seven days. After the seventh time, the people gave a loud shout, and the walls came tumbling down!

READ You will find this story in **Joshua chapter 6.**

Canaan - the Promised Lan

It was time for the Israelites to cross the River Jordan and go into the Promised Land. The river was deep and wide, and there were no bridges. How would they cross?

They were able to cross when God dried up the water for a short time. They made a pile of stones to remember what God had done for them.

The Canaanites

The Israelite armies went on to capture other parts of Canaan. They did not take all of the land in Joshua lifetime.

The Israelites had to learn to be farmers now, and to live in cities. Th land was divided up betwee the tribes, which were named after the sons of Jacob.

Land

God's own people

The God of Abraham wanted his people to be a **holy people**. 'Holy' means 'separate'. They were *meant* to be different from the Canaanites and the nations around them. Moses told them what would happen to them in Canaan:

Those people will turn your children away from me. Your children will begin serving other gods. The Lord will be very angry with you. And he will quickly destroy you. This is what you must

Some of the Israelites did not obey the laws that God gave them in the desert. They became like the Canaanites who did very bad things, like giving their children as sacrifices to the gods..

The Canaanites had always believed in many gods. They worshipped the rain god, Baal, because they thought if they did not please him, he would not send rain for their crops and they might starve. Some of the Israelites were tempted to worship Baal and other gods.

do to those people: tear down their altars. Smash their holy stone pillars. Cut down their Asherah idols and burn their idols in the fire. You are holy people. You belong to the Lord your God. He has chosen you from all the people on earth. You are his very own.

Deuteronomy 7:4-6

Now that they were living in the land that God had promised them, the Israelites had to remember everything Moses told them. They often had to be

reminded of all the things the Lord had done for them. Before Joshua died, he called all the people together and told them the whole story from Abraham to Moses and how God had brought them into the Promised Land.

Then Joshua told them:

"Now throw away the false gods that you have among you. Love the Lord, the God of Israel, with all your heart."
   Then the people said to Joshua, "We will serve the Lord our God. We will obey him."

Joshua 24:23,24

The Judges

When all those people who had been alive when Joshua was the leader had died, everything started to go wrong.

They did not know the Lord or what he had done for Israel. So they did evil and worshipped the Baal idols. They did what the Lord said was wrong. The Lord had brought the people of Israel out of Egypt. And the ancestors of these people had worshipped the Lord. But the Israelites stopped following the Lord. They began to worship the gods of the people who lived around them. That made the Lord angry.

Judges 2:10-12

Read Judges 2:16-19

The people told God they were sorry and asked him to save them. **SO . . .**

God chose a judge, who helped them to win. **BUT THEN**

The judge died **AND THEN**

The Israelites started to worship other gods. **SO . . .**

The Israelites worshipped other gods **SO**

When their enemies attacked them, they lost **SO**

Start here

Who were the Judges?

Judges were warriors who trusted God to help them win. Here are some you can read about:

Deborah

A wise woman who went to war against Jabin, the Canaanite king. She told a man called Barak to go, but he said,

Gideon

The Midianites rode camels and used to attack the Israelites and steal food from them. When the Lord told Gideon that he wanted him to fight the Midianites he replied,

I'll only go if you come with me

Of course I'll go with you. But you will not get credit for the victory

Judges chapters 4 and 5

Pardon me, Lord? How can I save Israel? My family group is the weakest, and I am the least important in my family.

Judges chapters 6 - 8

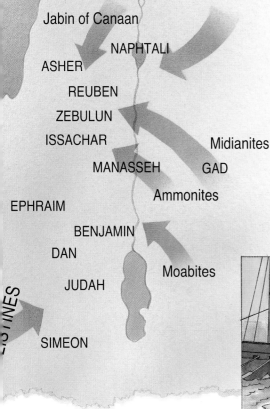

Jabin of Canaan
NAPHTALI
ASHER
REUBEN
ZEBULUN
ISSACHAR
MANASSEH
EPHRAIM
BENJAMIN
DAN
JUDAH
SIMEON

Midianites
GAD
Ammonites
Moabites

PHILISTINES

The Philistines.

The land to the west of Canaan, on the coast of the Mediterranean Sea, was taken over by 'sea people'. These people were called Philistines. They were already there when Israel came into the Promised Land. The Philistines grew into a strong nation and wanted more land. They wanted Canaan for themselves, and the Bible tells of many battles.

Samson

The **strong man** of the Bible. He fought with lions and defeated the Philistines. But he let himself be tricked by a woman.

When Samson told her his secret, he lost his strength, and he was captured by the Philistines.

Tell me why are you so strong?

Judges chapters 13 - 16

Ruth

Ruth is the book in the Bible which follows Judges. It tells a wonderful story about two poor women and how the Lord met all their needs. The younger woman, Ruth, married a man called Boaz. The Bible traces the family of King David back to them.

Samuel-
THE KINGMAKER

Samuel was the last of the Judges. He was also a prophet.

What's a prophet?

Well. if God speaks to you, and then you tell people what God said, you're a prophet.

Samuel's story begins before he was born. His father, Elkanah, had two wives.

Remember me! Don't forget me. If you will give me a son, I will give him back to you all his life.

Peninnah had children.

Hannah had no children.

So Hannah prayed to the Lord

God answered her prayer. Hannah gave birth to a son and named him Samuel.

Hannah kept her promise. When Samuel was about three years old, she took him to the Lord's Holy Tent at Shiloh. Hannah left him with Eli, the priest. Samuel grew up serving the Lord.

Read   **1 Samuel 1:21-28.**

Samuel was still very young when the Lord first spoke to him. You can read this story i **1 Samuel 3:1-21.**

Samuel became judge in Israel at a very troubled time. Israel was defeated in battle by the Philistines and the Holy Ark of God was taken away.

Samuel had two sons, and he made them judges in Israel. They were not good judges, and the people did not feel safe with them. So they said to Samuel

Give us a king to rule over us like all the other nations.

The Philistines soon sent the Holy Ark back to Israel - it gave them a lot of trouble. You can read about this in **1 Samuel chapter 5.**

(28)

Saul the first king

Samuel *anointed* Saul, making him king. Kings of Israel were anointed, to show that they were under the rule of God, who was the true King of Israel.

When Saul led the Israelites to victory over the Ammonites, the people believed that God had chosen him to be their king. He brought the tribes together into one nation.

King Saul was not a happy man. He often became angry. Music calmed him down, and the young shepherd boy, David, used to play the harp for him.

Saul did not always obey God. Samuel told Saul that God had turned against him, and he would lose the kingdom.

The Lord said to Samuel, "How long will you continue to feel sorry for Saul? I have rejected him as king of Israel. Fill your container with olive oil and go. I am sending you to Jesse who lives in Bethlehem. I have chosen one of his sons to be king.

1 Samuel 16:1

Samuel looked at seven of Jesse's sons, but the Lord told him, "I have not chosen any of these." So Samuel asked Jesse, "Are these all the sons you have?" The youngest son, David, who was looking after the sheep, was sent for.

The Lord said, "He is the one." Samuel poured the oil on David's head.

From that day on, the Lord's Spirit entered David with power.

1 Samuel 16:13

King David

While Saul was still alive, Samuel secretly anointed David king.

While David was very young, he killed the Philistine giant, Goliath, and became a great hero. You can read this story in **1 Samuel chapter 17.**

David became best friends with Jonathan - Saul's son.

Saul sent David to fight in different battles. And David was very successful. Then Saul put David over the soldiers. When he did this, Saul's officers and all the other people were pleased.

Women played instruments and danced in the streets. They sang,

**"Saul has killed thousands of his enemies.
But David has killed tens of thousands."**

1 Samuel 18:5-7

Saul became jealous of David and tried to kill him. Twice, David could have killed Saul, but he let him live, because he believed that God knew when the time was right for David to be king.

Saul and Jonathan died in a battle.

David and Bathsheba

Nathan was a prophet. He was not afraid of telling David the truth.

A rich man who had many sheep and cattle stole a lamb from a poor man.

That man must be punished for what he has done.

YOU are that man!

What had David done?

When David was a boy, he played the harp for King Saul. As a man, he wrote songs of prayer and worship. Some of these are in the book called Psalms. The best known is **Psalm 23**, which begins:

The Lord is my shepherd.
  I have everything I need.
He gives me rest in green
    pastures.
  He leads me to calm water.
  He gives me new strength.

and ends:

Surely your goodness and love
    will be with me
  all my life.
And I will live in the house of the
    Lord for ever.

Jerusalem

David captured the hill-town of Jerusalem from the Jebusites and made it the centre of government. He built himself a palace there.

The Holy Ark of God was brought to Jerusalem. David wanted to build a temple for the Lord, where the Holy Ark would stay, but the Lord did not want David to build it.

The Lord made a promise to David. He said,

"I took away my love and kindness from Saul. . . But your family and your kingdom will continue for ever before me. Your rule will last for ever.
2 Samuel 7:15,16

id saw Bathsheba, the ... of Uriah. He wanted ... for himself.

He gave orders that Uriah was to be sent to the most dangerous part of the battle.

Uriah was killed, and Bathsheba became David's wife.

Read 2 Samuel chapters 11 and 12. See what happened next. It's a sad story.

I have sinned against God!

Solomon-the temple

King David chose Solomon, the son of Bathsheba, to be the next king. Solomon was also God's choice. This is what God promised David:

"But, you will have a son. He will be a man of peace and rest. I will give him rest from all his enemies around him. His name will be Solomon. And I will give Israel peace and quiet while he is king. Solomon will build a temple for worship to me. He will be my son, and I will be his father. I will make his kingdom strong. Someone from his family will rule Israel for ever."

1 Chronicles 22:9-10

Solomon's wisdom

God asked the young King Solomon what he would like to have. In reply Solomon said he wanted the Lord to give him wisdom. He said,

"Without wisdom, it is impossible to rule this great people of yours."

1 Kings 3:9

God gave Solomon what he asked for, and Solomon became famous for his great wisdom. God said to him,

"Also, I will give you what you did not ask for. You will have riches and honor. . . I ask you to follow me and obey my laws and commands. Do this as your father David did. If you do, I will also give you a long life."

1 Kings 3:13-14

Read 1 Kings 3: 16-28

The Temple

Solomon became very rich and built splendid palace in Jerusalem, as wel as many other buildings.

The most important building was the Temple for the worship to the Lord i Jerusalem.

It took seven years to finish the building. Only the finest materials were used.

Bronze bowl fo the priests to was

It was a difficult problem, but Solomon knew how to find out the truth.

Solomon was the author of part of the book of **Proverbs**.

builder

The Holy Place
Read
1 Kings 7:48-50

The Most Holy Place
Read
1 Kings 6:19-28

The Holy Ark

The Altar

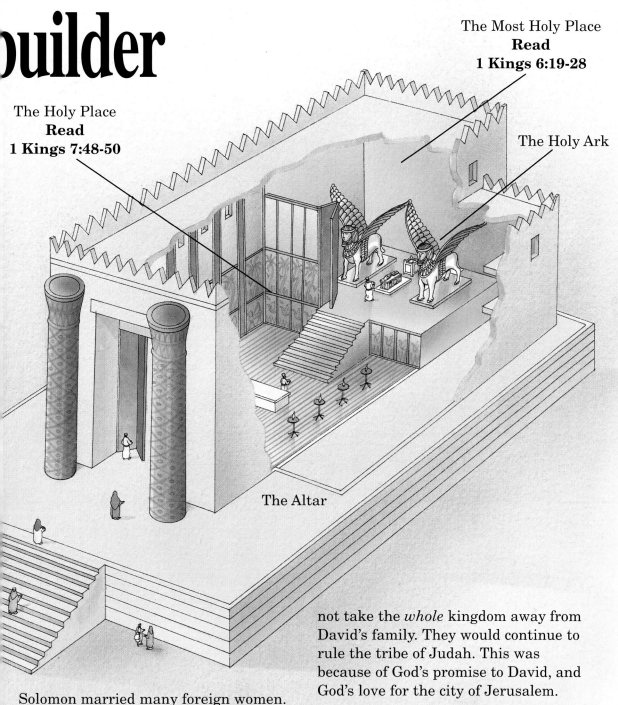

Solomon married many foreign women. They worshipped other gods. Because of this, Solomon did not obey the Lord's commands all his life.

God was angry with Solomon. He said,

"I promise I will tear your kingdom away from you. . . But I will not take it away while you are alive."
1 Kings 11:11,12

The Lord also promised that he would not take the *whole* kingdom away from David's family. They would continue to rule the tribe of Judah. This was because of God's promise to David, and God's love for the city of Jerusalem.

After Solomon's death, his son, Rehoboam, became king. The people rebelled against Rehoboam, because he was forcing them to work for him, like slaves in Egypt! The Israelites made Jeroboam their king.

The tribes of Judah and Benjamin in the south stayed loyal to the family of David.

The kingdom was divided!

Prophets and kings

Jeroboam was king of Israel, the ten tribes in the north. Many of his people were missing Jerusalem and the Temple. They wanted to worship God there.

In order to stop them going to Jerusalem, Jeroboam built two small temples, one in the north and one in the south.

But Jeroboam made a big mistake. In both places he built statues of bulls. These bulls were just like the ones the Canaanites put their idols on.

This encouraged the Israelites to worship idols, and break the laws that had been given by Moses.

God's messengers

The situation became very bad. In the 200 years that followed, Israel had 19 kings, and not one of them was a good king. They did not obey God's laws.

So God sent prophets to tell the kings and the people how to live better lives and turn back to the Lord.

Ahab was a very bad king. He married Jezebel, a Baal worshipper. Ahab built a temple for Baal.

There was no one like Ahab. No one had so often chosen to do what the Lord said was wrong. His wife Jezebel influenced him to do evil.

1 Kings 21:25

Elijah

Elijah was a man of God who showed the king and the people that God was powerful - and VERY angry!

Read 1 Kings 17:1-7

Elijah stops the rain.

No rain or dew will fall during the next few years unless I command it

Amos

The teachings of Amos were written down and will find these in your Bible.

Read Amos 2:6-7
Amos was a shepherd w lived at the time of King Jeroboam II. It was a ti of peace. The rich becar very rich, and the poor became very poor. Peop were so wicked, that th would even steal from t poor!

Read Amos 5:21-27
Amos saw the people

Read 2 Kings 5:1-19
This is the story of Naaman, who was healed of his leprosy.

n Israel

ad 1 Kings 18:21-39

This story shows us how powerful the Lord is, and how powerless Baal is. It's a bit like a competition - and God won!

Baal, answer us!

Lord, answer my prayer. Show these people that you, Lord, are God. Then the people will know that you are bringing them back to you.

EVENING. . .

...orshipping the Lord, but was all for show. Their ...earts were not in it.

...he Lord was angry with ...em for breaking the ...greement he made with ...em. God said he would ...unish them by giving ...eir enemies victory over ...em. Their enemies would ...en take them away to ...eir own country.

..., the Lord God, am ...atching the sinful ...ngdom Israel. ...will destroy Israel from ...e earth's surface."

Amos 9:8

Hosea

Hosea lived just after Amos. Even though he knew God was angry with Israel, Hosea, like Amos, looked forward to a better time. Hosea shows just how much the Lord loves his people.

**"The people of Israel will again live under my protection.
They will grow like the grain."**

Hosea 14:7

There had been no rain for three years. Then, it poured down!

The Lord is God! The Lord is God!

Read 1 Kings 18:41-46

ead 2 Kings 2:1-12

...he Bible tells us that Elijah ...d not die. He was taken up ... heaven in a whirlwind.

...lisha was Elijah's servant, ...d he was given the same ...wer that Elijah had.

Remember
Baal was supposed to be the god who controlled the weather!

The Southern

In 722 BC, the Northern Kingdom, Israel, was invaded by Assyria and the people were taken into exile.

The kings in Judah were all descendants of David. This is what God promised David. Some of these kings did not obey God. But there were four very good kings who led the people back into the ways the Lord wanted them to live.

You can read about these kings:

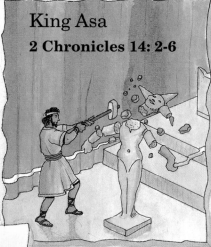

King Asa
2 Chronicles 14: 2-6

King Uzziah
2 Chronicles 26:9-10

King Hezekiah
2 Chronicles 29:27-30

King Josiah
2 Chronicles 34:29-32

Jonah was a prophet and the book with this name tells one of the best stories in the Bible! Jonah was swallowed by a giant fish! If you can't manage to read the whole story from the Bible, find it in a book of Bible stories.

Isaiah
Isaiah warned the people in Judah that the same thing would happen to them, as had happened to the people in the Northern Kingdom.

But Isaiah also looked forward to a time when God's people would return to their lands and be strong.

The Lord will again show mercy to the people of Jacob. The Lord will again choose the people of Israel. He will settle them in their own land.
Isaiah 14:1

Isaiah also wrote about the coming Messiah. [See page 41]

Kingdom

Micah lived in Judah at the same time as Isaiah. There were many bad prophets who told the people what they wanted to hear. But Micah was a prophet sent by God.

But the Lord's Spirit has filled me
with the power and strength to
preach fairness.
I will tell the people of Jacob how
they have turned against
God.
I will tell the people of Israel how
they have done wrong.

Micah 3:8

What had they done wrong?
Read Micah 3:9-11 to find out.

Nahum had a vision of how God would punish Assyria, the nation that attacked Israel and took the people away as slaves.

The destroyer is coming to
attack you, Nineveh.

Nahum 2:1

The prophets who lived in Judah had a difficult time trying to tell the people to obey God's laws. The bad kings were just as bad as the kings in Israel had been. Punishment would certainly come to Judah.

Jeremiah was a very unpopular prophet. People even tried to kill him. Jeremiah pleaded with the people to change their ways, return to God and obey his commandments.

But they would not listen. They went on worshipping other gods. The king did not help the poor and the needy people.

'Trouble will come to anyone who does not obey this agreement. I am talking about the agreement I made with your ancestors. I made it with them when I brought them out of Egypt . . . Obey me and do everything I command you. If you do this, you will be my people. And I will be your God. Then I will keep the promise I made to your ancestors. I promised to give them a land where much food grows.'

Jeremiah 11:3-5

In 586 BC the king of Babylon with his armies fought against Jerusalem and Judah, and destroyed the land and the cities. The people were taken away to Babylon. You can read what happened in **2 Chronicles 36:15-21.**

In a foreign land

Judah has gone into captivity.
  She has suffered and worked
    hard.
She lives among other nations.
  But she has found no rest.
Those who chased her caught her.
  They caught her when she was
    in trouble.

Lamentations 1:3

When King Nebuchadnezzar destroyed Jerusalem, he removed all the treasures from the Temple and took them back to Babylon with the people he captured.

You can see how bad it was for the people by reading Psalm 137.

By the rivers in Babylon we sat
    and cried when we
      remembered Jerusalem.
On the poplar trees nearby we
    hung our harps.
Those who captured us asked us
    to sing.
Our enemies wanted happy songs.
They said, "Sing us a Temple song
    from Jerusalem!"

But we cannot sing songs about
    the Lord while we are in
      this foreign country.

Psalm 137:1-4

Jeremiah went with them into exile and continued to prophesy among them. The book called **'Lamentations'** was probably written by Jeremiah in Babylon.

It was at about this time that the people of Judah became known as 'Jews'.

The story of Esther takes place in Susa at this time. It is the story of a Jewish girl who becomes a Persian queen, and saves her people from death.

Read Esther 9:18-19 and verse 22.
The Jewish festival of Purim is to celebrate the Jews' escape.

Habbakuk and Obadiah

Both these books were written during the exile. **Habbakuk** complained to God about the way the Babylonians treated the Jews. God shows how he has always been in control of history.

Obadiah had a vision that the Lord was going to punish the Edomites. Who were they? Remember Jacob's twin brother, Esau? The Edomites were Esau's descendants and were Israel's enemies.

Ezekiel was another prophet in the time of the exile. He had many dreams and visions which were messages from the Lord.

The most famous of Ezekiel's visions was the valley of dry bones. The Lord told him what to say to the bones:

Read Ezekiel 37:1-14

I will cause breath to enter you. Then you will live.

I will open up your graves and cause you to come up from them. And I will put my Spirit inside you. You will come to life. Then I will put you in your own land.

Daniel — Daniel chapter 3

This story takes place in Babylon, in the court of King Nebuchadnezzar. Daniel had three friends whose names were changed to Shadrach, Meshach and Abednego.

Nebuchadnezzar set up a golden statue which everyone had to worship. If they refused, they would be thrown into a blazing furnace.

But the Lord saved them from the fire

Our king, there are some men of Judah who don't obey your order - Shadrach, Meshach and Abednego.

Their God has sent his angel to rescue them. I now make this law. No one must speak against the God of Shadrach, Meshach and Abednego.

Another well known story is when Daniel was thrown into the lions' den. He broke the law by praying to God.
Read Daniel 6:16-28

Home to Jerusalem

The Jews were forced to stay in Babylon for about 50 years. When Nebuchadnezzar died, Babylon was quickly captured by Cyrus of Persia. The Persian Empire was very large, and Cyrus wanted all exiled people to return to their own countries.

Not all the Jews wanted to go home, but some did return to Jerusalem, taking with them the Temple treasures. They started to rebuild the Temple, but did not carry on with the work.

Haggai, the prophet, said this in 520BC:

"The Temple is still in ruins. Is it right for you to be living in fancy houses?"

Haggai 1:4

'Work, because I am with you', says the Lord of heaven's armies. 'I made a promise to you when you came out of Egypt. My Spirit is still with you. So don't be afraid.'

Haggai 2:4,5

Ezra and Nehemiah

These books tell the story of the rebuilding of Jerusalem.

Read Ezra chapter 4 to find out why the people became afraid of building the Temple. You will also see how the problem got sorted out.

Ezra himself returned to Jerusalem 60 years after the Temple was completed. The walls of the city were still in need of repair.

Ezra was a scholar and teacher. He led the Jews back to the Lord's ways.

Ezra opened the book. All the people could see him because he was above them. As he opened it, all the people stood up. Ezra praised the Lord, the great God. And all the people held up their hands and said, "Amen! Amen!" Then they bowed down and worshipped the Lord with their faces to the ground.

Nehemiah 8:5,6

Nehemiah was still in Babylon when he heard that the walls of Jerusalem were still broken down. It made him very sad. The king sent him back to Jerusalem to help rebuild the walls and gates.

Read Nehemiah 2:11-18 to see what Nehemiah did when he arrived in Jerusalem.

Under Nehemiah's guidance, the walls of the city were rebuilt in 52 days. The enemies of the Jews tried to stop them, but Nehemiah prayed, and the work was completed. He said:

Our enemies were trying to scare us. They were thinking, "They will get too weak to work. The wall will not be finished." But I prayed, "God, make me strong."

Nehemiah 6

The last two books in the Old testament are the prophets **Zechariah** and **Malachi.**

Like Haggai, **Zechariah** encouraged the people in Jerusalem to rebuild the Temple. God promised:

"I will protect my Temple from armies who come and go. No one will hurt my people again because now I am guarding it"
Zechariah 9:8

Malachi wrote after the work in Jerusalem was finished. His message was for the priests, who were not obeying God.

Promises for the future

After the Jews returned to their own land, no more of their history is found in the Bible. Another 400 years passed before the birth of Jesus.

The Jews continued to be ruled by foreign powers. After the Persian Empire came the Greek Empire under Alexander the Great. After an uprising led by Judas Maccabaeus, they had their own rulers for 80 years. This was not a peaceful time, and the Romans took over in 63BC.

But the prophets looked forward to a time when God would give them a king from the family of David.

A child will be born to us.
God will give a son to us.

He will rule as king on David's throne
and over David's kingdom.
Isaiah 9:6-7

This king would be different from any other king they had known.

Your king is coming to you.
He does what is right, and he saves.
He is gentle and riding on a donkey.
Zechariah 9:9

A new agreement

Jeremiah wrote,

"Look, the time is coming," says the Lord,
"when I will make a new agreement.
I will make this agreement with the people of Israel,"
says the Lord.
"I will put my teachings in their minds.
And I will write them on their hearts.
I will be their God,
and they will be my people."
Jeremiah 31:31,33

With these promises in their minds, the Jews had a great hope that they would be saved from their enemies and life would be better for them.

They had a name for the one who was coming -

The Messiah!

Songs, Poems..

Job
Psalms
Proverbs
Ecclesiastes
Song of Songs

If you hold up your Bible, and open it in a place just before the middle, you will probably find yourself reading a **Psalm.** The Book of Psalms is a collection of songs.

There are songs that praise the Lord for who he is, and what he has done.

There are songs of sadness.

There are 'prayer songs'.

King David wrote many of the Psalms.

Music and dancing

As well as singing, many musical instruments were used for worship. You can find some of these in **Psalm 150.**

There was a lot of dancing in worship too.

Job

Before Psalms you will find the book of Job [say 'Jobe'].

Poor Job suffered much. Everything went wrong for him, but he went on trusting God.

There has always been suffering in the world, and people always ask why this should be, when the Bible says that God loves us. Job's story does not answer this question,

Ecclesiastes

> **Useless! Useless! Completely useless! All things are useless.**
> *Ecclesiastes 1:2*

The writer was a wise man, but he found it hard to make sense of life. So much seemed pointless to him. Many people feel like this today too.

Read Ecclesiastes 11:7-10 to find some good, practical advice for young people.

Read Psalm 51
When David saw that he had done wrong, he was very sorry, and wanted to change.

Read Psalm 23
Pictures of shepherds and sheep are often used to show how good God is to his people.

and Wise Words

ut it helps people when
hey are hurting. If Job
an go on trusting God,
nyone can.

ob is one of the 'Wisdom'
ooks. The others are
cclesiastes and
roverbs. In these books
e find questions about
fe, and suggestions for
ving a good life.

Proverbs

Proverbs is a very easy
book to read. There is
lots of advice about
living sensibly. If you
want to know how to
have a happy life, read
some verses from
Proverbs every day.

Read Proverbs 14:1-9
Find four things that a
wise person will do. And
four things that a foolish
person will do.

Where does wisdom come
from?

> **Only the Lord gives wisdom.
> Knowledge and understanding
> come from him.**
> *Proverbs 2:6*

Read Proverbs 31:10-31
This is a poem in praise
of a good wife.

onour God and obey his
commands.
his is the most important
thing people can do.
od knows everything
people do, even the things
done in secret.
e knows all the good and all
the bad.
e will judge everything
people do.
Ecclesiastes 12:13-14

> *My darling,
> you are beautiful!*

> *You are so
> handsome, my lover*

Song of Songs

This is a love poem, written by
Solomon.

Palestine in the time of

The Romans joined together the countries that are known in the Old Testament as Israel, Judah and Philistia, with other countries nearby. They called this region **Palestine.**

The region around Jerusalem is called **Judea** in the New Testament.

Galilee

About 100 years before the birth of Jesus, Galilee, a territory in the north, was conquered by the Jews. All the non-Jews there had to obey the Jewish laws.

The Samaritans

Between Judea and Galilee was a region known as Samaria. Samaritans were hated by the Jews. If Jews traveled between Galilee and Judea, they did not take the fast route through Samaria if they had time to go the long way round!

The town, Samaria, became the capital of the Northern Kingdom. This town became famous for idol worship.

The Samaritans of Jesus' time were descended from Israelites who stayed in the Northern Kingdom after the exile and married the foreigners who came to live among them.

The Roman Empire.

The Romans ruled the whole of the civilised world. The people enjoyed a long time of peace, though they did not like being under Roman rule. They had to pay high taxes. Some Jews worked for the Romans as tax collectors.

Read Luke 19:1-9
The story of a tax collector!

Travel was easy along the Roman roads, and most people could speak Greek. Messages traveled fast, so the Good News about Jesus would spread very quickly around the known world.

The Romans let the Jews have local 'kings' to govern them. The best known of these was Herod the Great. He was hated by the Jews, but he tried to make himself popular by building a new temple in Jerusalem.

Zealots

These were people who wanted the Jews to be free from Roman rule. They organised riots and acted like terrorists. They believed that the Messiah, when he came, would be a powerful king who would lead them to victory over the Romans.

Jesus

Pharisees and Sadducees

The Pharisees loved the law. They tried to obey every detail of the Old Testament laws, and added lots of rules of their own.

Read Mark 2:23-28.
The Pharisees worried about things that did not matter. They did not approve of Jesus and his followers. The Pharisees did not believe Jesus could be the Messiah.

The Sadducees came from priestly families. They were very rich and important men. They believed the first five books of the Old Testament [the Laws of Moses] but disagreed with the Pharisees. Sadducees did not believe that dead people would be raised from death. They also argued with Jesus.

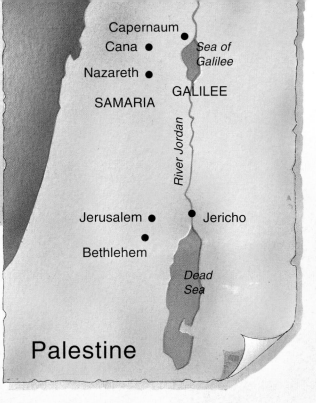

Palestine

We were living against God, but at the right time, Christ died for us.

Romans 5:6

Jesus came at the right time in history.

The law was given through Moses, but grace and truth came through Jesus Christ. No man has ever seen God, but God the only Son is very close to the Father. And the Son has shown us what God is like.

John 1:17-18

Palestine

Roman Empire

Good News!

The Gospels of Matthew, Mark, Luke and John all tell us about the life of Jesus. The people who had been with Jesus remembered all the things he had said and done, and everything that had happened. They talked about these things to other people all the time. When Jesus' followers had grown old, the stories needed to be written down.

Luke explains why he is writing about the life of Jesus to his friend, Theophilus.

Read Luke 1:1-4

The prophet Isaiah lived 700 years before Jesus was born. He had good news for God's people.

A child will be born to us.
God will give a son to us.

. . . **Power and peace will be in**
his kingdom.
It will continue to grow.
He will rule on David's throne
and over David's kingdom.

Isaiah 9:6,7

Jesus is born

God sent the angel Gabriel to a young woman called Mary. Mary lived in Nazareth. She was engaged to be married to Joseph, a carpenter.

Don't be afraid, Mary, because God is pleased with you. You will become pregnant. You will give birth to a son, and you will name him Jesus.

He will rule over the people of Jacob for ever. His kingdom will never end.

How will this happen? I am a virgin!

The Holy Spirit will come upon you, and the power of the Most High will cover you. The baby will be called the Son of God.

Meanwhile, at Joseph's house

I will divorce her secretly.

Joseph, don't be afraid to take Mary as your wife. The baby in her is from the Holy Spirit. She will give birth to a son. You will name the son Jesus. Give him that name because he will save his people from their sins.

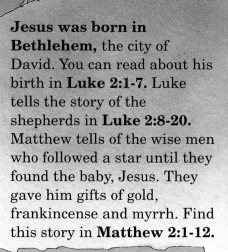

Jesus was born in Bethlehem, the city of David. You can read about his birth in **Luke 2:1-7.** Luke tells the story of the shepherds in **Luke 2:8-20.** Matthew tells of the wise men who followed a star until they found the baby, Jesus. They gave him gifts of gold, frankincense and myrrh. Find this story in **Matthew 2:1-12.**

John the Baptist

Before John was born, an angel told his father,

"He will help many people of Israel return to the Lord their God. He himself will go first before the Lord . . . He will make people ready for the coming of the Lord."

Luke 1:16,17

Read Matthew 3:1-6

Verse 1 - What did John the Baptist do? Where?

Verse 2 - What did he say?
Verse 4 - What did he wear? What did he eat?

Verse 6 - What did John the Baptist do with people in the Jordan River?

When Jesus became a man, he went to John to be baptized. The Holy Spirit came down on Jesus. It was like a dove. And then a voice from heaven said,

This is my Son and I love him. I am very pleased with him.
Matthew 3:17

The Kingdom

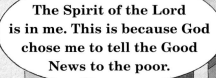

Luke tells us that after Jesus was baptised he went to Galilee. He began to teach in the synagogues, and people liked him. Then Jesus went back to his home in Nazareth.

Jesus stood up in the synagogue in Nazareth and read from the prophet Isaiah:

> The Spirit of the Lord is in me. This is because God chose me to tell the Good News to the poor.

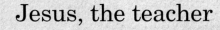

> God sent me to tell the prisoners of sin that they are free, and to tell the blind that they can see again.

Jesus, the teacher

Everywhere Jesus went, large crowds gathered to hear him teach about the kingdom of God. People loved to listen to Jesus, and their lives were changed by what they heard.

The gospel writers tell us many of the things that Jesus taught. Today people's lives can still be changed by the teaching of Jesus.

Where is the Kingdom of God?

This is a question people asked Jesus. The Jews were waiting for their Messiah to come. They thought that this leader, when he came, would set them free from the rule of the Romans.

Jesus gave this answer to the question:

"God's kingdom is coming, but not in a way you will be able to see with your eyes. People will not say, 'Look, God's kingdom is here!' or 'There it is!' No, God's kingdom is within you."
Luke 17:20,21

God's kingdom is the rule of God in people's hearts and minds. This is how the world can become what God meant it to be when he first created it.

# of God

God sent me to free those who have been treated unfairly, and to announce the time when the Lord will show kindness to his people.

Luke 4:18,19

The people of Nazareth were very angry with Jesus. They did not believe that he was the Christ.

Read Matthew 5:17-20

The importance of the law
Jesus told people that they must obey the law that God gave Moses.

Read Matthew 6:25-34

Don't worry
If you care about God's kingdom, then God will give you everything you need.

The Good News by MATTHEW

Matthew wrote his Gospel to show the Jews that Jesus was the Messiah they had been waiting for.

Read Matthew 7: 24-29

The two houses
If you hear AND obey the words of Jesus, then you will be a wise person.

The Sermon on the Mount

This is the title that has been given to the teachings of Jesus found in Matthew chapters 5, 6 and 7. It has this name because Jesus went up on a hill to speak to the people.

Follow Jesus

Mark **was the first Gospel to be written.** Mark wrote for the Christians in Rome, so they would know how to follow Jesus. Matthew and Luke used Mark's gospel to help them write theirs.

Luke **is the only gospel writer who was not a Jew.** He was a Greek doctor. Luke also wrote the book of Acts - the story of the early church.

12 special followers

Wherever Jesus went in Galilee, many people followed him. But Jesus chose 12 special followers, and called them 'apostles'.

These special followers were also known as 'disciples'. They would be the ones to tell everyone the Good News about the kingdom of God after Jesus died.

Parables

When Jesus was teaching people or answering their questions, he often told a story. These stories were called 'parables'. They were about ordinary life and they help us to understand about the kingdom of God.

Read
Luke 15:3-7

Read
Luke 15:8-

Chief priests, scribes and Pharisee.

Many tax collectors and "sinners" came to listen to Jesus. The Pharisees and teachers of the law began to complain: "Look! This man welcomes sinners and even eats with them!"

Luke 15:1-

Read Mark 1:16-20 and see how Simon, Andrew, James and John became Jesus' special followers. The others were Philip, Thomas, Bartholomew, Matthew, James [the son of Alphaeus], Simon the Zealot, Judas [the son of James] and Judas Iscariot.

Jesus called the 12 apostles together. He gave them power over all demons. Jesus sent the apostles out to tell about God's kingdom and to heal the sick.

Luke 9:1,2

Have you ever lost something that you like very much, and then you searched for it and found it? If so, you will understand the stories about the lost sheep, the lost coin and the lost son.

Read Luke 15:11-32

That's a miracle!

In the gospels we read many stories of miracles that Jesus did. A miracle is something that doesn't happen naturally.

Some of these miracles were just to do people good - they were sick and Jesus made them well again. Other miracles showed that Jesus had power over God's created world.

Read Mark 1: 40-45.
This man had leprosy, a very bad skin disease. Lepers had to live apart from other people, who were scared they would catch the disease. Jesus healed many lepers.

Read Luke 9:10-17.
This is the story of the feeding of the 5,000. How many loaves and fishes were there to eat?

The religious leaders hated Jesus. They did not like the way he taught the people about the kingdom of God. They did not want to believe that Jesus was the Messiah, sent by God. The chief priests wanted to kill Jesus.

Believe in Jesus

John tells us exactly why he wrote his Gospel:

. . . so that you can believe that Jesus is the Christ, the Son of God. Then, by believing, you can have life through his name.

John 20:31

John's Gospel is different from the other three, even though he tells many of the same stories. He gives a lot more space to Jesus' teaching.

I am

When God told Moses to go back to Egypt and free the Israelites from slavery, Moses asked, "Who shall I say sent me?" God said,

"Tell them, 'I AM sent me to you'.

Exodus 3:14

The words "I AM" in the Old Testament are a sort of 'code' for the name of God. When Jesus used "I AM" to talk about himself, he was telling the people that he was the Son of God.

Jesus said,

I am the bread that gives life. He who comes to me will never be hungry. He who believes in me will never be thirsty.

John 6:35

I am the light of the world. The person who follows me will never walk in darkness. He will have the light that gives life.

John 8:12

I am the door. The person who enters through me will be saved. . . I came to give life - life in all its fullness.

John 10:9,10

I am the good shepherd. The good shepherd gives his life for the sheep.

John 10:11

In John's Gospel Jesus says a lot about himself. He wants us to know who he is, where he comes from, and what he will do for us.

When John writes about miracles, he wants the reader to understand that what Jesus did shows us that he is the Son of God.

Read John 5:1-17

Jesus healed a man, but the Jewish leaders were not happy because he did this on the Sabbath day. What Jesus said to the leaders made them very angry.

"First Jesus was breaking the law about the Sabbath day. Then he said God is his own Father! He is making himself equal with God!"

John 5:18

I am the way. And I am the truth and the life. The only way to the Father is through me.

John 14:6

I am the resurrection and the life. He who believes in me will have life even if he dies.

John 11:25

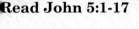

I am the vine, and you are the branches. If a person remains in me and I remain in him, then he produces much fruit.

John 15:5

'Resurrection' is a dead person coming back to life. In John 11:38-45 Jesus brought his friend Lazarus back to life. Jesus did this to show people that he was sent by God. Jesus also prepared them for his own resurrection.

Jesus died . . .

Jesus said,

"I am the good shepherd. The good shepherd gives his life for the sheep. . .
. . . The Father loves me because I give my life. I give my life so that I can take it back again. No one takes it away from me. I give my own life freely."

John 10:11,17,18

Jesus spoke to his followers many times about his death.

He explained that the older Jewish leaders, the leading priests, and the teachers of the law would make him suffer many things. And he told them that he must be killed. Then on the third day he would be raised from death.

Matthew 16:21

You can read about the death of Jesus in all four Gospels. Start by reading Mark's story.

Mark 14:1,2

The Jewish leaders plotted to kill Jesus.

Mark 14:12-26

Jesus and his followers ate the Passover meal together.

This bread is my body. Take it.

This is my blood which begins the new agreement that God makes with his people.

Mark 15:1-20

The leading priests took Jesus to the Roman Governor - Pilate. Pilate could not find anything wrong with Jesus, but the Jewish leaders wanted to have him killed.

Mark 15:21-32

Jesus was taken away by soldiers and killed on a cross.

When Jesus died, the curta in the Temple split into two pieces.

Mark 15:

and rose again!

Hundred's of years before these things happened, the prophet Isaiah wrote:

But he was wounded for the wrong things we did.
He was crushed for the evil things we did.
The punishment, which made us well, was given to him.
And we are healed because of his wounds.

Isaiah 53:5

Mark 14:43-65

Jesus was arrested and brought before the High Priest.

This curtain divided the Most Holy Place from the other part of the Temple. God was in the Most Holy Place, and only the high priest was allowed to go in there - once a year to offer a sacrifice for the sins of God's people. When Jesus died he became the sacrifice for the sins of the whole world. Now anyone can come close to God - and there is no more need for animal sacrifices.

Read Mark 15:42-47

Jesus' body was laid in a tomb - a hole cut out of a rock - and a large stone was rolled over the hole.

See what happened next. Find John's story - **John 20:1-18.**

Mary Magdalene went to the tomb and found the stone had been rolled away. She looked inside - the body had gone! Two angels were sitting there.

She thought the man outside was the gardener, and when he said her name, 'Mary', she knew it was Jesus! He had risen from death, just as he said he would.

Read Matthew 28:16-20

Before Jesus went back to his Father in heaven, he told his followers to go and tell the whole world the Good News about the kingdom of God. He told them to teach the people and to baptize them.

Tell the World!

Mark ends his Gospel with these words:

The followers went everywhere in the world and told the Good News to people. And the Lord helped them. The Lord proved that the Good News they told was true by giving them power to work miracles.

Mark 16:20

The fifth book in the New Testament is called 'Acts' - meaning 'Acts of the apostles'; that is, all the things the apostles did. The writer is Luke. Read his introduction - **Acts 1: 1-5.**

The Holy Spirit

When the day of Pentecost came, they were all together in one place. Suddenly a noise came from heaven. It sounded like a strong wind blowing. The noise filled the whole house where they were sitting. They saw something that looked like flames of fire. The flames were separated and stood over each person there. They were all filled with the Holy Spirit, and they began to speak different languages. The Holy Spirit was giving them the power to speak these languages.

Acts 2:1-4

Peter's speech

There were many Jews in Jerusalem who had come for Pentecost, the feast to celebrate the summer harvest. They thought the followers of Jesus were drunk.

Peter stood up and spoke to the crowd. He told them the whole story about Jesus, and how only Jesus could be the one the prophets wrote about.

READ Acts 1:6-11

Jesus was taken up into heaven. The apostles saw him go. Before he left them Jesus said,

The Holy Spirit will come to you. Then you will receive power. You will be my witnesses . . . in every part of the world.

Acts 1:8

READ Acts 2:22-

What shall we do?

Change your hearts and lives and be baptized, each one of you, in the name of Jesus Christ for the forgiveness of your sins.

And you will receive the gift of the Holy Spirit.
Acts 2:38

3,000 people were baptized that day and added to the group of believers. Every day more people believed in Jesus and the church grew.

Miracles

The apostles were doing many miracles and signs.

Acts 2:43

Peter healed a crippled man. You can read this story in **Acts 3:1-10**.

The Jewish leaders were very unhappy about the growing numbers of believers.

Peter and John were put in jail. The Jewish leaders told them not to speak or teach in the name of Jesus, but they could not punish them,

Read Acts 4:32-35

The believers shared everything they owned.

because all the people were praising God for what had been done.

Acts 4:21

Trouble for the believers

Trouble started when some Jews told lies against one of the leaders in the church, a man called Stephen.

Stephen made a long speech. He told the whole Bible story from Abraham, Moses and David, right up to Jesus. But Stephen made the Jewish leaders angry when he said,

You stubborn Jewish leaders! You have not given your hearts to God! You won't listen to him! You are always against what the Holy Spirit is trying to tell you.

Acts 7:51

Stephen was stoned to death. After this the Jews made the believers suffer very much. Most of the Christians left Jerusalem.

And everywhere they were scattered, they told people the Good News.

Acts 8:4

Watching in the crowd, when Stephen was stoned, was a man named Saul.

Saul was also trying to destroy the church. He went from house to house. He dragged out men and women and put them in jail.

Acts 8:3

Good News for Jews...

At first, the Good News about Jesus was told only to the Jews.

But the Lord showed Peter that the Good News was for everyone.

Read Peter's story in **Acts 11:5-17**. See how the gift of the Holy Spirit was given to non-Jewish people.

Thessalon
Philippi
Troas
Rome
Corinth
CR
MALTA
Mediterranean Sea

Saul

Remember the man who was watching when Stephen was stoned? Saul was on his way to Damascus to arrest as many followers of Jesus as he could and bring them back to Jerusalem when he met Jesus. **Read Acts 9:3-19**

Saul! Saul! Why are you doing things against me?

Who are you Lord?

I am Jesus. I am the One you a trying to hurt.

Go! I have chosen Saul for an important work.

He must make me known to non-Jews, to kings, and to the people of Israel.

Brother Saul, the Lord Jesus sent me. He sent me so you could see again, and be filled with the Holy Spirit.

nd Greeks

Paul's missionary journeys

Paul traveled all over the Roman Empire telling the Good News about Jesus. He started churches in the towns he visited. These churches grew, and when Paul was not with them, he wrote them letters. Many of these letters are in the New Testament and we can learn a lot from them about living the Christian life.

The last journey of Paul that we read about in Acts, was his journey by boat to Rome. Paul was taken to Rome as a prisoner, where he was allowed to live in his own house, with guards. He was able to preach the Good News and give encouragement to the church there. Rome was the centre of government and trade, and from this city, the Good News would spread through the whole world!

Antioch

Lystra

esus

CYPRUS

Tyre

Caesarea

aul got up and went to Damascus. He was blind. Three days later, the Lord spoke to a man named Ananias.

Ananias!

Here I am, Lord.

Lord, many people have told me about this man and the terrible things he did to your people in Jerusalem.

Get up and go to the street called Straight Street. Ask for a man named Saul from the city of Tarsus.

few days later . . .

Jesus is the Son of God.

Saul? Paul?

Saul spoke Greek and used the Greek name, Paul, when he was with non-Jewish people. He calls himself 'Paul' in all the letters he wrote to the churches, so we call him 'Paul'.

Paul's

The letters of Paul to the churches, and to his friends were written BEFORE the Gospels. They were copied and passed around the churches because the believers could learn so much from these letters.

Lessons to learn

When Jesus was on earth, he spent a lot of time teaching his followers. He told the apostles that one of the things they would have to do was to TEACH the new followers - all the people who would believe in Jesus when they had not even seen him.

In the churches there were Jews who knew the Jewish scriptures, what we now call the 'Old Testament'. There were also non-Jewish people who did not know anything about the Jewish law. They did not know how God made himself known to people before he sent his Son, Jesus, into the world. They also had strange ideas which came from other religions.

Paul and the other apostles often had to correct the new believers when they did not understand things properly.

A lazy lot!

Paul told the church in Thessalonica that Jesus was going to return. So some people thought they need not bother to work any more! Paul had to tell them off!

We hear that some people in your group refuse to work. They do nothing. And they busy themselves in other people's lives. We command those people to work quietly and earn their own food.

2 Thessalonians 3:11,12

'Be strong.'

This is what Paul said to the Colossians:

As you received Christ Jesus the Lord, so continue to live in him. Keep your roots deep in him, and have your lives built on him. Be strong in the faith, just as you were taught.

Colossians 2:6,7

Letters

The Church in Rome

Paul had not been to Rome when he wrote his letter to the church. He was looking forward to going there.

This letter could be called 'The Good News by Paul'. He explains how sin came into the world through Adam, and how God sent Jesus to bring people back to himself.

We have been made right with God because of our faith.

Romans 5:1

We have been made right with God by the blood of Christ's death . . . Through Jesus we are now God's friends again.

Romans 5:9,11

Pleasing God

In all his letters, Paul gives lots of good advice to believers.

Help each other with your troubles. When you do this, you truly obey the law of Christ.

Galatians 6:2

Be full of joy in the Lord always.

Philippians 4:4

Children, obey your parents the way the Lord wants.

Ephesians 6:1

Tell the rich people to do good and to be rich in doing good deeds.

1 Timothy 6:18

Living the

The letter to the Hebrews

We do not know who wrote this letter, but it was written for Jews who had accepted Jesus as their Messiah. They knew the Old Testament, and the writer shows them all the teaching about Jesus in the Old Testament. The whole Bible tells us about Jesus.

Some of these people were close to giving up believing in Jesus, and the letter encourages them to keep going in their faith.

Faith means being sure of the things we hope for. And faith means knowing that something is real even if we do not see it.

Hebrews 11:1

Read Hebrews chapter 11 to see how men and women in the Bible kept their faith in God.

James

James wrote this letter to Christians everywhere to teach them the right way to live. Faith is important, but it's no good to anyone if good works do not follow.

A person might think he is religious. But if he says things he should not say, then he is just fooling himself. Religion that God accepts is this: caring for orphans or widows who need help; and keeping yourself free from the world's evil influence.

James 1:26,27

The letters of Peter

These letters were written by Peter, the Apostle of Jesus.

But we saw the greatness of Jesus with our own eyes.

2 Peter 1:16

So much of what Peter

wrote in his letters is based on his own experiences and on things he had learned from his many mistakes!
He said,

Always be ready to answer everyone who asks you to explain about the hope you have.

1 Peter 3:15

This was Peter - the same man who said he did not know Jesus!
Read Matthew 26:31-35, and 69-75

Jude's letter warns about false teachers. It is similar to what Peter writes in 2 Peter chapter 2.

The letters of John

Many Christians suffered, and some were even killed, on the orders of Roman Emperors who wanted everyone to worship images of themselves, along with

Christian life

ne Roman gods. It was
hard time for the
hurch. John wrote:

**rothers, do not be
urprised when the
eople of this world
ate you. We know that
e have left death and
ome into life. We know
his because we love
ur brothers in Christ.**
1 John 3:13-14

ut the real enemies of
he church were the
alse teachers and those
n the church who did
ot believe God's true
eaching.

**hey refuse to say that
esus Christ came to
arth and became a
nan.**
2 John:8

ike Peter, John was a
ollower of Jesus. His
etters were written to
emind Christians of the
ruth. Revelation, the
ast book in the Bible,
vas also written by
ohn.

The end times

The Bible promises that Jesus will
return.

**Look, Jesus is coming with the clouds!
Everyone will see him, even those who
stabbed him. And all peoples of the earth
will cry loudly because of him. Yes, this
will happen! Amen.**
    **The Lord God says, "I am the Alpha
and the Omega. I am the One who is and
was and is coming. I am the All-
Powerful."**
Revelation 1:7,8

John was in prison on the island of
Patmos near the end of the first century.
Jesus gave John this revelation, which
John wrote down for 'The Seven
Churches'. These churches are named in
Revelation chapters 2 and 3.

Revelation is not an easy book to read or
understand. John had seen a vision of
Jesus glorified. God showed him things
that would happen in the future. How
God would judge the world and evil
would be destroyed for ever.

Read Revelation 22:1-5

**Jesus is the One who says that these
things are true. Now he says, "Yes, I
am coming soon."**
    Amen. Come, Lord Jesus!
Revelation 22:20

Revelation

Index